THE POLLINATOR'S CORRIDOR
a graphic novel

VOLUME
ONE

Aaron Birk

Black Willow Productions
Philadelphia, 2011

www.thepollinatorscorridor.com

"The Pollinator's Corridor"
Volume One
Aaron Birk

First
Edition

published 2011 by
Black Willow Productions

© AaronBirk 2011

ISBN: 978-0-615-56291-9
Black Willow Productions

P.O. Box 19347   Philadelphia, PA 19143
Printed in the United States of America

Aaron Birk maintains exclusive rights to all work in this book. Sale, reproduction or distribution of any artwork and images herein is prohibited by law. For more information on subsequent editions or to request permission to use images from this book, please contact the author.

WITH GENEROUS FINANCIAL SUPPORT FROM

The Independence Foundation
The Greater Philadelphia Cultural Alliance
New York Foundation For The Arts

And Individual Support from:
Ann Birk, Asher Auel, Shimon Schwartzchild, Anna Baker,
Bruce Schimmel, Tony Larson, Michael and Jane Swirsky,
Peter and Pat Levitin, Rob and Cindy Aden, Larry and Diane Climo,
Merril and Barbara Climo, Marjorie and Michael Wilder,
David and Elana Levitin

AND INSTITUTIONAL SUPPORT

Bronx Museum of the Arts
The Philadelphia City Paper
The University of Illinois Urbana-Champaign
The Wagner Free Institute of Science
The Eastern Apiculture Society
The Philadelphia Bee Keepers Guild
Urban Nutrition Initiative
Norton Island Residency for Artists and Writers
Byrdcliffe Guild Artist In Residence Program
The Rotunda
Studio 34 Yoga
Bronx River Alliance

PRODUCTION ASSISTANCE

Matt Walsh, Dina Kelberman, Ron Lipsky, Fran Staret,
Emily Zeitlyn, Philip, Joel, and Jeff Eckel of We Bee Brothers

ALSO SPECIAL THANKS TO

Carolyn Huckabay, Dr. May Barenbaum, Lauren Zalut,
Suzanne Matlock, Kristin Schwab, Sergio Bessa, Anna Herman,
Tasha Doremus, Jim Bobb, Vincent Aloyo,
Graeme McHenry, Mathew Brown,
Ana Opitz, Myra Bazell,
Regina Alvarez, Kevin Matteson,
Carol Maxwell, Leslie Sauer, author of
"The Once and Future Forest"
The Society for Ecological Restoration

Thanks to U.S. Geological Survey
Department of the Interior/USGS
for permission to modify and reproduce
topographic maps of New York from
the 7.5 minute series.

To my family Ann, Peter, Dan and Jenn

to

Shimon
Schwartzchild

and to
my Grandpa

Dr. Sam Climo

he would have
liked this

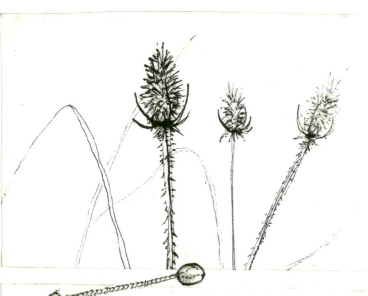

the NATURALIST's tools ARE CURIOSITY, OBSERVATION, AND THE ABILITY TO MAKE CONNECTIONS. YOU WILL DEVELOP A WORKING KNOWLEDGE OF OUR REGION'S INLAND AND COASTAL ECOLOGY, INVESTIGATING CLIMATE VARIANCE, SUCCESSION THEORY, AND THE EVOLUTION OF SPECIES. YOU WILL ADDRESS CRITICAL ISSUES IN NUTRIENT-TRANSPORT, SOIL AND WATER CONSERVATION, AND HABITAT LOSS.

IN ORDER TO SUCCEED YOU MUST LEARN TO OPEN YOUR SENSES AND THINK FREELY.

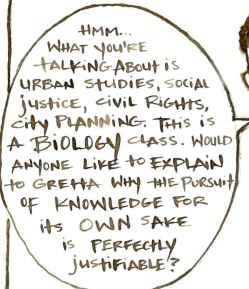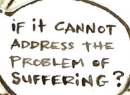

25

chapter two

"knight of the saltmarsh"

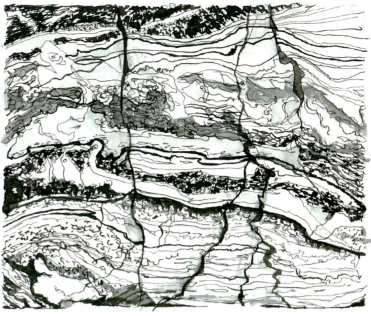

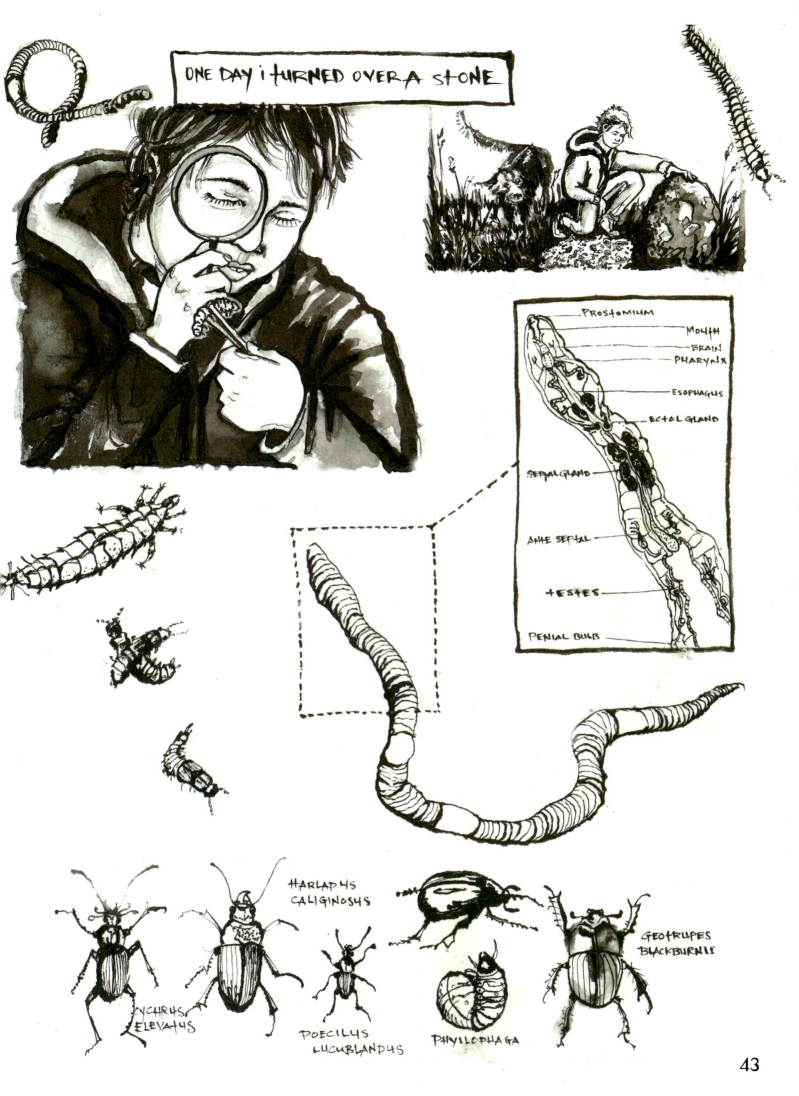

HEY GRETTA, DO YOU THINK THE TIDES WILL BE OUT LONG ENOUGH TO STAKE DOWN EROSION LOGS? I FORGOT THE— WHAAAAAT? NO.. HOLY GOD, GRETTA I KNOW THIS BIKE LAST NIGHT... I SAW IT IN MY DREAM. HE WAS SOME KIND OF MAIL-COURIER PRIEST.

HE HAD A LEATHER MAIL-BAG AND AN OLD BRITISH MOTORBIKE, IT WAS THIS BIKE...

HE WAS A SIKH, I BELIEVE, AND RUNNING OUT OF TIME. BUT STILL, HE SET DOWN HIS LOAD, TOOK OFF HIS SHIRT, AND BATHED IN THE ESTUARY. IT WAS RIGHT HERE.

AND IT WAS CLEAR TO ME, THAT **ALL** HE EVER DID WAS PRAY, AND ALL HE EVER PRAYED FOR WAS PEACE.

These highways were raised from my bones... But what you and I both know is that under this toxic rug there is a seed who's tough. Coating the water will crack. And when the wisteria grows over my power lines and climbs the steel girders of my arms and legs... well, THAT'S when you can flinch.

Yo what planet are you on? Look around you. Where do you think you ARE? Sam, just listen for a while, ok? Once this project is done and you get to graduate, I still gotta live here, I gotta EAT this. The walls between us, they were built before we were born. And the South Bronx was built on my body.

"Sun's gettin' high, eh? Whew! So, what you're saying is... you ARE the Bronx. Right? And that... since it burned, and took ol' one-eyed Satchel with it, I mean, your GRANDfather, no one was there to... um... But WHY did it burn?"

"Ok, Sam. It goes like this: In Satchel's day, folks brought mattresses to the roof, played steel-string in the streets. No one locked their door because everyone had a job. Canning, textiles, and cabinetry brought food to the table.

The South Bronx had iron foundries. It had a PIANO FACTORY! But by the 1950's the Fed got into "urban renewal," replacing entire blocks with giant storage containers for the poor. In the 1960's banks started red-lining the South Bronx, barring investment.

Working class whites fled to the suburbs, just in time for the Cross-Bronx Expressway to gouge our neighborhoods and cut us off from the water. By 1970 a third of the industries were gone, taking 17,000 jobs with them. Cafés, drugstores and grocers were taxed out of town and the ones left behind got ROBBED. Libraries closed. Then heroin appeared. Public safety collapsed. Assaults and burglaries overwhelmed our one precinct, known as "FORT APACHE." Landlords sold their buildings to eviction agencies

Until at last the gutted, windowless hulks could be stripped for copper, doused in gasoline and torched. Insurance money flowed. Between 1970 and 1975 there were 68,456 fires, about 30 a night.

Momma once took me to a crater on Burnside Ave and said "Look between the cracks. This is where your grandpappy used to live.""

...r & ripping old dead trees,

we cable their corpses to the bank, building in-stream structures to SLOW THE FLOW, AND

RE-DIRECT THE CURRENT.

We roped-in the after school crowd. "Are bi-valve mollusks classified as benthic invertebrates?" WELL, UHHH...

These kids are masters of data collection; they "sein" for aquatic species, fish, crabs, and crustaceans, record the numbers AND LET THEM GO.

We contend with riparian-corridor infringements, channel aggradation, floating garbage... these are structural concerns. But there are deeper problems here. Estuarine fish, oysters, mussels, and phytoplankton — the whole aquatic food web — depends on dissolved oxygen. But impervious surfaces force rain to the gutter, carrying shit from under your car; this is called "non-point source pollution." Combined sewer outflows and hundreds of illegal discharge pipes deliver billions of gallons of raw sewage, which is basically nitrogen, FERTILIZER.

High bacteria loads and ALGAL BLOOMS use up the oxygen, causing mass die-offs of fish and plankton... It looks like HIJIKI SALAD!

DEPTHS WITHIN DEPTHS... AND WHAT LURKS? WHEN RAINDROPS FALL WHO SWIMS THE SILT, THE ROILING SEDIMENT, UNDER BASE-FLOW TURBULENCE AND SURFACE CURRENTS? WHO RIDES THE SALT-WEDGE, WHERE FRESH WATERS MEET THE OCEAN-BRINE? TO COMBAT IGNORANCE WE MEASURE TURBIDITY, SALINITY, PH AND DISSOLVED OXYGEN. AND THEN COMES THE REAL TEST: SHOVING LIVE CORDGRASS INTO THE SLOP.

NOW, SPARTINA, TAKE BACK THIS BRACKISH PLACE, SLOW RUNOFF AND STABILIZE FLOODS, CAPTURE STORMWATER AND INFILTRATE THE SOIL, GROWING AND DECAYING, PILING ON TOP OF YOURSELF IN DENSELY-ROOTED BOG-MATS, TO BE POCK-MARKED BY BURROWING INVERTEBRATES, FIDDLER CRABS, A LOBSTER OR TWO...

AND HARK! WHAT MIGRATORY BIRDS PLUCK MUSSELS FROM THE MUD, TO SHOW OFF A CLOUD AND SHATTER THEM ON THE ROCKS? LET MINE EYES BE GREETED BY THE SNOWY EGRET, THE SWALLOW-TAIL, WHITE GULLS AND CORMORANTS, AND WHO WOULD HAVE THOUGHT "SALT-HAY" COULD SAVE US ALL?

The day has been a watershed of fresh energy. Sometimes you just have to stop what you are doing, lean on your shovel, and take in the scene.

See the barnacles? Those clumps of kelp and alaria? How about that family wagon floating past?

And now, as the sky grows old, all the tired players start winding down...

And all at once, like anadromous fish returning to the sea, they are GONE.

But for me a plan begins to SMOLDER..

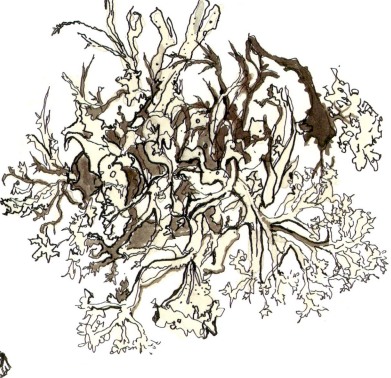

I'd like to stabilize this whole hydrologic network. To one day engineer a continuous network of ground-water exchange in the channel, to build in-stream habitat, eliminate combined sewer outflow, and capture rainwater.

But Gretta aint smiling. I think she knows what we're both unwilling to say: it's too big for us, the wound too deep, that torrent of problems too far over our heads.

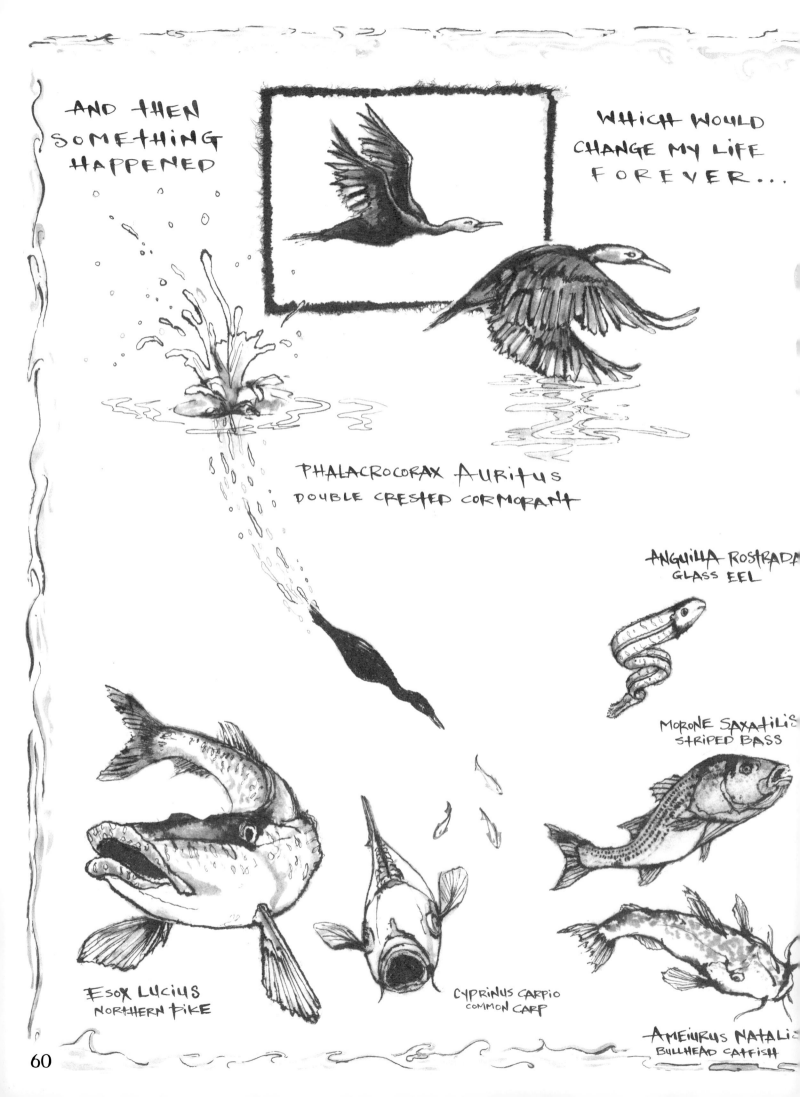

AND SO...
We huffed the dripping basket upshore, across the street, and to the IRON STAIRCASE. At first GRETA refused to come, but when the TRAIN ARRIVED, she RELENTED.

"LISTEN, BARKER: this is MY PROJECT too. If you want to recruit some DERELICT, international, runaway VAGABOND i Ain't gonna wait around for your bloated CORPSE to float down the RIVER. You wanna carry some FISH to whatever WASTE land this cat calls HOME? You're damn RIGHT i'm coming... i gotta PROTECT your ass."

...AND SO...
WE RODE THE METAL SNAKE.

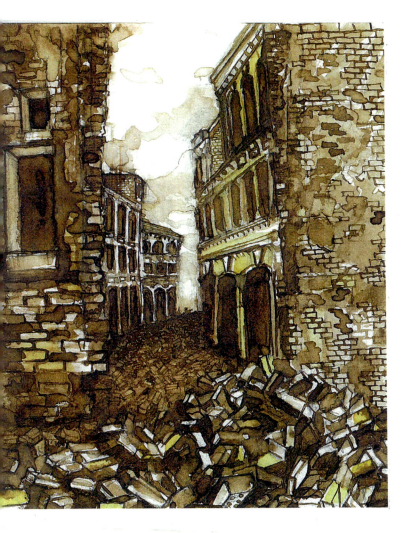

This was the journey to Natasha's squat, and these were the old-world corridors... I didn't know there were still places like this, with stones that could speak. I sensed that we had left New York, to navigate the bombed-out streets, the gutted husks and abandoned lots, the rusting fire escapes and corroded roofs of a forgotten world.

We followed the stranger. Here were the strata of buried generations, exposed layers of the families who had lived here. There were the Jews and the Irish, the Blacks and the Puerto Ricans... there were the Dutch,

And before them the Lenape, elders of all Algonquian peoples.

With her basket of fish weighing heavily, I marched on, while Gretta tredded softly behind, watching every crevice for a pair of eyes. Until at last we came to a door.

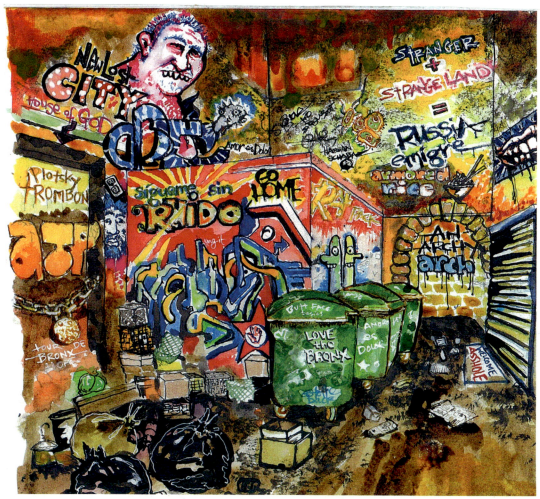

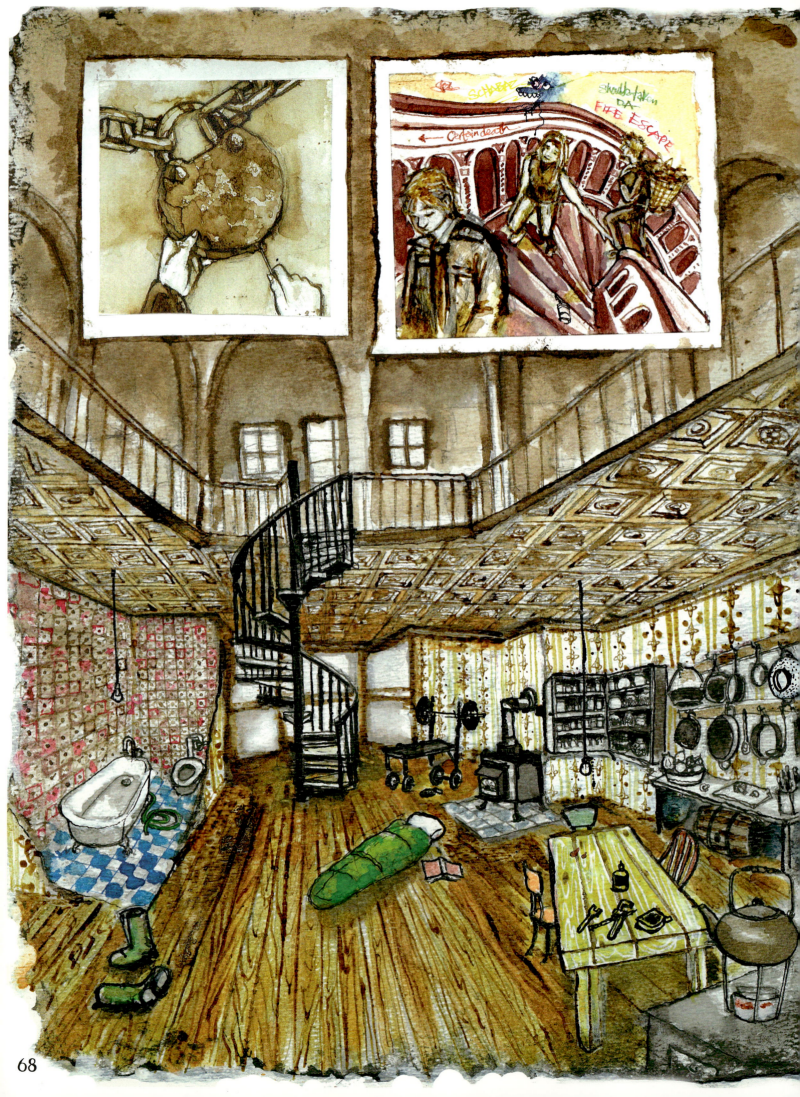

"I'M LISTENING, SAM."

THIS ONE'S BIGGER THAN US, GRETHA. IT'S BIGGER THAN DR. BENZING'S CLASS AND IT'S BIGGER THAN THE BRONX. IN ANCIENT TIMES YOU COULD WALK BAREFOOT ON THE ECTOMYCHORRIZAE, PEEL WEBBY MYCELIA FROM THE FOREST FLOOR... WHO KNOWS, 125TH ST. COULD HAVE BEEN A SAVANNAH, JEROME AVENUE A WETLAND, GLACIAL TILL AND ROCK FLOUR KICKING UP DUST IN THE ICY WINDS...

CUT TO THE CHASE, SAM.

YOU GOT A MAP?

i see WEEDS growing through the cracks, and those VERY cracks WIDENED by children with CROWBARS. we meet LIVING and NON-LIVING systems with the ecology of our bodies.

chapter three

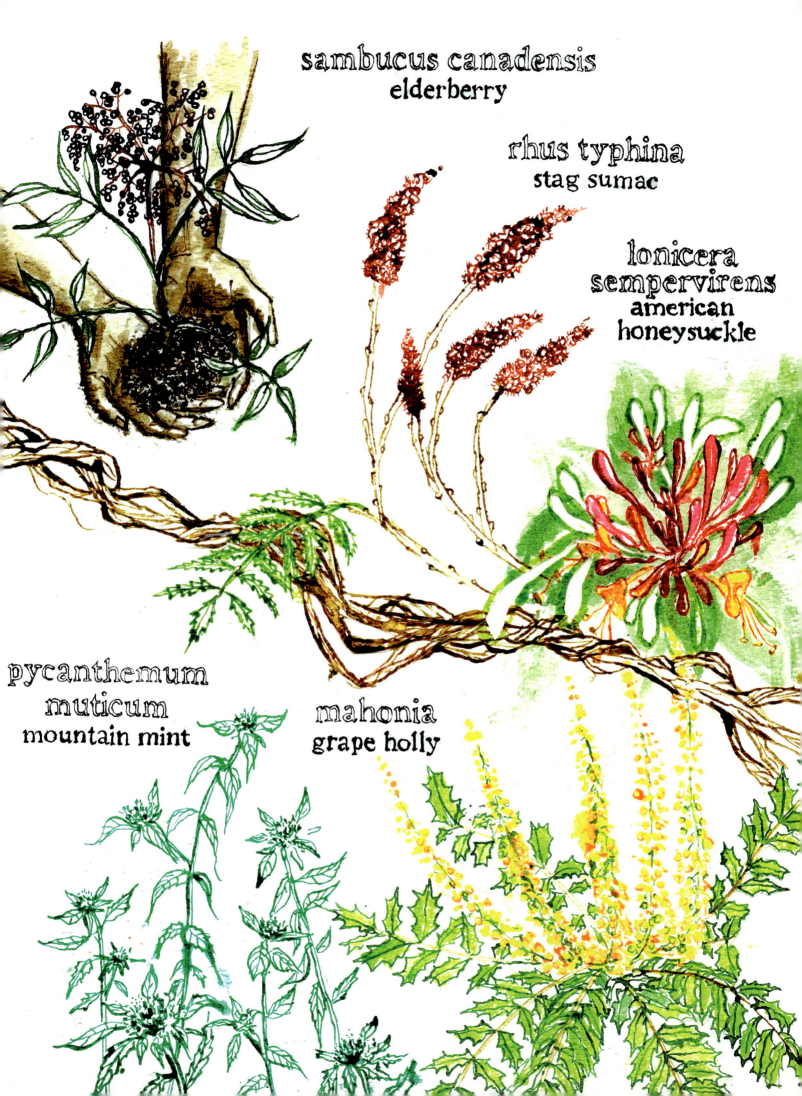

to be continued...

Eastern Apicultural Society of North America

Annual Conferences

EAS 2012
August 13-17, 2012
Burlington, VT

EAS 2013
August 5-9, 2013
West Chester, PA

Hands-On Courses in Beekeeping
Lectures, Workshops & Family Programs
Delivered by Nationally and Internationally Known Experts

Topics may include:

- **Making Peace & Places for Honey Bees**
- **More Bees; Better Bees**
- **All Pollinators Considered**
- **Bees – the Gift that Keeps Giving**
- **A Forager's Challenge: Nutrition and Pesticides**
- **Landscape Ecology for Sustainable Beekeeping**
- **Innovative Partnerships, Home and Abroad**

PLUS Social & Networking Opportunities:
- Wednesday Picnic
- Friday Banquet
- Field Trips
- Vendor and Exhibitor Space available for your business or organization

Come experience the wonder of the small but mighty honey bee!
For more information visit www.easternapiculture.org

EAS
Eastern Apicultural Society